Mother Teresa

1910–1997

IN THE HEART

of

THE WORLD

Thoughts, Stories, & Prayers

MOTHER TERESA

Edited by Becky Benenate

NEW WORLD LIBRARY
NOVATO, CALIFORNIA

New World Library
14 Pamaron Way
Novato, California 94949

Cover design: Big Fish
Photographs: Michael Collopy
Text design: Aaron Kenedi
Chapter opening quotes reprinted by permission from
Works of Love are Works of Peace by Michael Collopy,
published by Ignatius Press, San Francisco, California.

Originally published as *The Mother Teresa Reader, A Life for God*,
compiled by LaVonne Neff, which was derived from works compiled
and edited by Henry Dietrich, Jose Luis Gonzalez-Balado, and
Angelo Scolozzi, published by Servant Publications, Inc., © 1995.
This edition copyright © 1997 by New World Library.

Library of Congress Cataloging-in-Publication Data

Teresa, Mother, 1910 – 1997
[Mother Teresa reader]
In the heart of the world : thoughts, stories, & prayers
Mother Teresa : edited by Becky Benenate
p. cm.
originally published: Mother Teresa reader.
Servant Publications, ©1995.
ISBN 1-57731-065-9 (cloth : alk. paper)
1. Meditations. I. Benenate, Becky. II. Title.
BX2182.2.T3965 1997   97-149
248.4'82—dc21   CIP

First printing, October 1997
Printed in U.S.A. on acid-free paper
Distributed by Publishers Group West

10 9 8 7 6 5 4 3 2 1

CONTENTS

～

PART I.　　～ THOUGHTS

On Compassion 11

On Silence 17

On Joy 25

On Contemplation 31

On Generosity 37

On Sacrifice 45

PART II.　　～ STORIES

Remember the Small Things 53

The Distressing Disguise of Suffering 55

Giving Freely 57

To Notice Beauty in Others 59

Opening the Heart 61

To Die Like an Angel 63

Abandonment Is an Awful Poverty 65

The Warmth of a Hand 67

To Give of Yourself 69

Sharing Love with Others 71

The Great Gift of Love 73

The Tenderness of God 75

A Home, A Gift 77

A Beautiful Example of Love 79

Generous and Great People 81

PART III. ∾ PRAYERS

Make Me an Instrument of Your Peace 87

Shine Through Me 89

Blessed Are You Among Women 93

With Deep Gratitude 95

Holy, Holy, Holy 97

Our Father 99

Come, Let Us Bow Down 103

O Jesus, You Who Suffer 105

IN THE HEART

of

THE WORLD

Thoughts

On Compassion

~~

"We will never know how much
just a simple smile will do."

et us not use bombs and guns to overcome the world. Let us use love and compassion. Peace begins with a smile. Smile five times a day at someone you don't really want to smile at at all. Do it for peace. Let us radiate the peace of God and so light His light and extinguish in the world and in the hearts of all men all hatred and love for power. Smile at one another. It is not always easy. Sometimes I find it hard to smile at my Sister, but then I pray.

God loves the world through you and through me. Are we that love and that compassion? Christ came to be his Father's compassion. God is loving the world through you and through me and through all those who are His love and compassion in the world.

There is much suffering in the world — very much. Material suffering is suffering from hunger, suffering from homelessness, from all kinds of disease, but I still think that the greatest suffering is being lonely, feeling unloved, just having no one. I have come more and more to realize that it is being unwanted that is the worst disease that any human being can ever experience.

In these times of development, the whole world runs and is hurried. But there are some who fall down on the way and have no strength to go ahead. These are the ones we must care about.

Let us be very sincere in our dealings with each other and have the courage to accept each other as we are. Do not be surprised at or become preoccupied with each other's failure; rather see and find the good in each other, for each one of us is created in the image of God. Jesus has said it beautifully: "I am the vine, you are the branches." The life-giving sap that flows from the vine through each of the branches is the same.

～

Be kind in your actions. Do not think that you are the only one who can do efficient work, work worth showing. This makes you harsh in your judgment of others who may not have the same talents. Do your best and trust that others do their best. And be faithful in small things because it is in them that your strength lies.

The Gospels remind us that Jesus, before he taught the people, felt compassion for the multitudes that followed after him. Sometimes he felt it even to the point of forgetting to eat. How did he put his compassion into practice? He multiplied the loaves of bread and the fish to satisfy their hunger. He gave them food to eat until they couldn't eat any more, and twelve full baskets were left over. Only then did he teach them.

In loving one another through our works we bring an increase of grace and a growth in divine love.

On Silence

~~~

"Yesterday is gone.
Tomorrow has not yet come.
We have only today,
Let us begin."

In the silence of the heart God speaks. If you face God in prayer and silence, God will speak to you. Then you will know that you are nothing. It is only when you realize your nothingness, your emptiness, that God can fill you with Himself. Souls of prayer are souls of great silence.

There is a very holy priest, who is also one of the best theologians in India right now. I know him very well, and I said to him, "Father, you talk all day about God. How close you must be to God!" And you know what he said to me? He said, "I may be talking much *about* God, but I may be talking very little *to* God." And then he explained, "I may be rattling off so many words and may be saying many good things, but deep down I do not have the time to listen. Because in the silence of the heart, God speaks."

~~~

We cannot put ourselves directly in the presence of God if we do not practice internal and external silence.

In silence we will find new energy and true unity. Silence gives us a new outlook on everything.

The essential thing is not what we say but what God says to us and through us. In that silence, He will listen to us; there He will speak to our soul, and there we will hear His voice.

Listen in silence because if your heart is full of other things you cannot hear the voice of God. But when you have listened to the voice of God in the stillness of your heart, then your heart is filled with God.

The contemplatives and ascetics of all ages and religions have sought God in the silence and solitude of the desert, forest, and mountains. Jesus himself spent forty days in the desert and the mountains, communing for long hours with the Father in the silence of the night.

We too are called to withdraw at certain intervals into deeper silence and aloneness with God, together as a community as well as personally. To be alone with him — not with our books, thoughts, and memories but completely stripped of everything — to dwell lovingly in his presence, silent, empty, expectant, and motionless. We cannot find God in noise or agitation.

In nature we find silence — the trees, flowers, and grass grow in silence. The stars, the moon, and the sun move in silence.

Silence of the heart is necessary so you can hear God everywhere — in the closing of a door, in the person who needs you, in the birds that sing, in the flowers, in the animals.

What is essential is not what we say but what God tells us and what He tells others through us. In silence He listens to us; in silence He speaks to our souls. In silence we are granted the privilege of listening to His voice.

To make possible true inner silence, practice:

Silence of the eyes, by seeking always the beauty and goodness of God everywhere, closing them to the faults of others and to all that is sinful and disturbing to the soul;

Silence of the ears, by listening always to the voice of God and to the cry of the poor and the needy, closing them to all other voices that come from fallen human nature, such as gossip, tale-bearing, and uncharitable words;

Silence of the tongue, by praising God and speaking the life-giving Word of God that is the Truth, that enlightens and inspires, brings peace, hope, and joy, and by refraining from self-defense and every word that causes darkness, turmoil, pain, and death;

Silence of the mind, by opening it to the truth and knowledge of God in prayer and contemplation, like Mary who pondered the marvels of the Lord in her heart, and by closing it to all untruths, distractions, destructive thoughts, rash judgments, false suspicions of others, revengeful thoughts, and desires;

Silence of the heart, by loving God with our heart, soul, mind, and strength and one another as God loves, and avoiding all selfishness, hatred, envy, jealousy, and greed.

～

I shall keep the silence of my heart with greater care, so that in the silence of my heart I hear His words of comfort and from the fullness of my heart I comfort Jesus in the distressing disguise of the poor. For in the silence and purity of the heart God speaks.

On Joy

⁓

*"Like Jesus, we belong to the whole world,
living not for ourselves but for others.
The joy of the Lord is our strength."*

A joyful heart is the normal result of a heart burning with love. Joy is not simply a matter of temperament, it is always hard to remain joyful — all the more reason why we should try to acquire it and make it grow in our hearts.

Joy is prayer; joy is strength; joy is love. She gives most who gives with joy.

To children and to the poor, to all those who suffer and are lonely, give them always a happy smile; give them not only your care but also your heart. We may not be able to give much, but we can always give the joy that springs from a heart that is filled with love.

If in your work you have difficulties and you accept them with joy, with a big smile, in this, like many other things, you will see your good works. And the best way to show your gratitude is to accept everything with joy.

～

If you are joyful, it will shine in your eyes and in your look, in your conversation and in your contentment. You will not be able to hide it because joy overflows.

Joy is very contagious. Try, therefore, to be always overflowing with joy wherever you go.

Joy, according to St. Bonaventure, has been given to man so that he can rejoice in God because of the hope of the eternal good and all the benefits he receives from God. Thus he will know how to rejoice at his neighbor's prosperity, how to feel discontent concerning empty things.

Joy must be one of the pivots of our life. It is the token of a generous personality. Sometimes it is also a mantle that clothes a life of sacrifice and self-giving. A person who has this gift often reaches high summits. He or she is like a sun in a community.

We should ask ourselves, "Have I really experienced the joy of loving?" True love is love that causes us pain, that hurts, and yet brings us joy. That is why we must pray and ask for the courage to love.

∽

May God give back to you in love all the love you have given and all the joy and peace you have sown around you, all over the world.

On Contemplation

～

"Seeking the face of God in everything, everyone,
everywhere, all the time, and seeing His hand in every
happening — that is contemplation
in the heart of the world."

By contemplation the soul draws directly from the heart of God the graces that the active life must distribute.

We [the Missionaries of Charity] are called to be contemplatives in the heart of the world by:

Seeking the face of God in everything, everyone, everywhere, all the time, and his hand in every happening;

Seeing and adoring the presence of Jesus, especially in the lowly appearance of bread, and in the distressing disguise of the poor.

Our life of contemplation must retain the

following characteristics:

Being missionaries: by going out physically or in spirit in search of souls all over the world.

Being contemplatives: by gathering the whole world at the very center of our hearts where the Lord abides, and allowing the pure water of divine grace to flow plentifully and unceasingly from the source itself, on the whole of His creation.

Being universal: by praying and contemplating with all and for all, especially with and for the spiritually poorest of the poor.

Another aspect of our life of contemplation is simplicity, which makes us see the face of God in everything, everyone, everywhere, all the time, and His hand in all the happenings; and makes us do all that we do — whether we think, study, work, speak, eat, or take our rest — under the loving gaze of the Father, being totally available to Him in any form He may come to us.

What is contemplation? To live the life of Jesus.

This is what I understand — to love Jesus, to live His life in us, to live our life in His life. That's contemplation. We must have a clean heart to be able to see: no jealousy, anger, contention, and especially no uncharitableness.

~~~

To me, contemplation is not to be shut up in a dark place but to allow Jesus to live His passion, love, and humility in us, praying with us, being with us, sanctifying through us.

On Generosity

~⁀

*"Every act of love is a work of peace,
no matter how small."*

There are many medicines and cures for all kinds of sick people. But unless kind hands are given in service and generous hearts are given in love, I do not think there can ever be any cure for the terrible sickness of feeling unloved.

It may happen that a mere smile, a short visit, the lighting of a lamp, writing a letter for a blind man, carrying a bucket of charcoal, offering a pair of sandals, reading the newspaper for someone — something small, very small — may, in fact, be our love of God in action. Listening, when no one else volunteers to listen, is no doubt a very noble thing.

Holiness grows fast where there is kindness. I have

never heard of kind souls going astray. The world is lost for want of sweetness and kindness.

～

We need money, medicines, clothing, and a thousand other things for the poor we serve. If so many people weren't generous, thousands would be left unaided. Because we still have many poor, needy children and families that live in the streets — not only in Calcutta but in London, Rotterdam, Madrid, Marseilles, and Rome — the need is great. In the last city I mentioned, we have many needy. The sisters go out at night into the streets, especially around the train station, between 10 P.M. and 2 A.M. to pick up the homeless and take them to the home we have on San Gregorio al Cielo.

The last time that I was in Rome, I found it unbearable to see so many homeless people living that way. So I went to see the mayor of Rome and said, "Give me a place for these people, because they refuse to come with us and would rather stay where they are." He and his staff responded wonderfully. In a few days they offered us a very nice place near the Termini Train Station. At present, all those who have nowhere else to spend the night except in the streets go there and sleep in beds. In the morning they leave.

This is the wonderful part of our vocation, that as Missionaries of Charity we have created an awareness of the poor in the whole world. Twenty years ago no one would have believed that there were hungry, naked men and women around. Today the whole world knows our poor because of our work. And they want to share.

Why is our congregation known all over the world today? It is because people see what we do: feeding the hungry, clothing the naked, taking care of the sick and the dying. Because they see, they believe.

～

I am convinced that today's youth are more generous than those of times past. Our youth are better prepared and more willing to sacrifice for the service of man. For that reason, it is no surprise that young people have a preference for our congregation. To a large extent these are young people from the middle class. They have everything: wealth, comfort, high status. However, they ask to enter a congregation that is at the service of the poor, in order to lead a life of real poverty and contemplation.

Sometimes the rich seem very willing to share in their own way the unhappiness of others. But it is a pity that they never give to the point of feeling that they are in need.

The present generations, especially children, understand better. There are English children who make sacrifices in order to be able to offer a muffin to our children. There are Danish children who make sacrifices in order to be able to offer others a glass of milk every day. And German children do the same in order to be able to offer the poor some fortified food.

These are concrete ways of teaching love. When these children grow up, they will know what it means to give.

～○

There are many people who can do big things, but there are very few people who will do the small things.

On Sacrifice

"Love, to be real, must cost —
it must hurt — it must empty us of self."

Sacrifice is at the heart of Christian faith. The people of God in Old Testament times offered animals for their sins — lambs, goats, bulls, and pigeons. Jesus offered himself as a perfect, final sacrifice so that the animal sacrifices would not have to be repeated.

Sacrifice, surrender, and suffering are not popular topics nowadays. Our culture makes us believe that we can have it all, that we should demand our rights, that with the right technology all pain and problems can be overcome. This is not my attitude toward sacrifice. I know that it is impossible to relieve the world's suffering unless God's people are willing to surrender to God, to make sacrifices, and to suffer along with the poor.

From the beginning of time the human heart has felt the need to offer God a sacrifice. What is an acceptable sacrifice? One that is good for the people of God. One that is made on behalf of the world.

～

There are lonely people around you in hospitals and psychiatric wards. There are so many people who are homeless! In New York City, our sisters are working among the destitute who are dying. What pain it causes to see these people! They are only known by their street address now. Yet they were all someone's children. Someone loved them at one time. They loved others during their lifetime. But now they are only known by their street address.

The words of Jesus, "Love one another as I have loved you," must be not only a light for us but a flame that consumes the self in us. Love, in order to survive, must be nourished by sacrifices, especially the sacrifice of self.

Suffering is nothing by itself. But suffering shared with the passion of Christ is a wonderful gift, the most beautiful gift, a token of love.

～

I must be willing to give whatever it takes to do good to others. This requires that I be willing to give until it hurts. Otherwise, there is no true love in me and I bring injustice, not peace, to those around me.

Stories

Remember the Small Things

⁓

Some of my sisters work in Australia. On a reservation, among the Aborigines, there was an elderly man. I can assure you that you have never seen a situation as difficult as that poor old man's. He was completely ignored by everyone. His home was disordered and dirty.

I told him, "Please, let me clean your house, wash your clothes, and make your bed." He answered, "I'm okay like this. Let it be."

I said again, "You will be still better if you allow me to do it."

He finally agreed. So I was able to clean his house and wash his clothes. I discovered a beautiful lamp, covered with dust. Only God knows how many years had passed since he last lit it.

I said to him, "Don't you light your lamp? Don't you ever use it?"

He answered, "No. No one comes to see me. I have no need to light it. Who would I light it for?"

I asked, "Would you light it every night if the sisters came?"

He replied, "Of course."

From that day on the sisters committed themselves to visiting him every evening. We cleaned the lamp, and the sisters would light it every evening.

Two years passed. I had completely forgotten that man. He sent this message: "Tell my friend that the light she lit in my life continues to shine still."

I thought it was a very small thing. We often neglect small things.

The Distressing Disguise
of Suffering

～

$\mathcal{I}$ remember one of our sisters, who had just gradu-
ated from the university. She came from a well-to-
do family that lived outside of India.

According to our rule, the very next day after
joining our society, the postulants must go to the
home for the dying destitute in Calcutta. Before this
sister went, I told her, "You saw the priest during the
Mass, with what love, with what delicate care he
touched the body of Christ. Make sure you do the
same thing when you get to the home, because Jesus is
there in a distressing disguise."

So she went, and after three hours, she came back. That girl from the university, who had seen and understood so many things, came to my room with such a beautiful smile on her face. She said, "For three hours I've been touching the body of Christ!"

And I said, "What did you do? What happened?"

She said, "They brought a man from the street who had fallen into a drain and had been there for some time. He was covered with maggots and dirt and wounds. And though I found it very difficult, I cleaned him, and I knew I was touching the body of Christ!"

She knew!

⁓

Hungry for love, He looks at you. Thirsty for kindness, He begs of you. Naked for loyalty, He hopes in you. Homeless for shelter in your heart, He asks of you. Will you be that one to Him?

Giving Freely

⚫

At a seminary in Bangalore, a nun once said to me, "Mother Teresa, you are spoiling the poor people by giving them things free. They are losing their human dignity."

When everyone was quiet, I said calmly, "No one spoils as much as God himself. See the wonderful gifts he has given us freely. All of you here have no glasses, yet you all can see. If God were to take money for your sight, what would happen? Continually we are breathing and living on oxygen that we do not pay for. What would happen if God were to say, 'If you work four hours, you will get sunshine for two hours?' How many of us would survive then?"

Then I also told them, "There are many congregations that spoil the rich; it is good to have one congregation in the name of the poor, to spoil the poor."

There was profound silence; nobody said a word after that.

～

To Notice Beauty in Others

～

One year I wanted to do something special for our sisters. I sent out a newsletter to each one of them, to each community, suggesting that each one write down what she thought was beautiful in her sisters and her community. I asked that each sister send her answer to me.

A thousand letters arrived. Just imagine! I had to sit down and read each one, making a list of each community and all the sisters. Later I returned the letters to the communities.

The sisters were surprised that someone would

notice such beautiful things in them — that there was someone who was able to see them. All of this fostered a beautiful spirit of love, understanding, and sharing.

I feel that we too often focus on the negative aspects of life, on what is bad. If we were more willing to see the good and the beautiful things that surround us, we would be able to transform our families. From there, we would change our next-door neighbors and then others who live in our neighborhood or city. We would be able to bring peace and love to our world, which hungers so much for these things.

Opening the Heart

~~~

One day, we picked up a man off the street who looked like a fairly well-to-do person. He was completely drunk. He couldn't even stand up because he was so drunk!

We took him to our home. The sisters treated him with love, care, and kindness.

After a fortnight, he told the sisters, "Sisters, my heart is open. Through you I have come to realize that God loves me. I've felt His tender love for me. I want to go home." And we helped him get ready to go home.

After a month, he came back to our home and gave the sisters his first paycheck. He told the sisters, "Do to others what you have done to me." And he walked away a different person.

Love had brought him back to his family, to his children's tenderness, to his wife's understanding love.

Let us ask Our Lady to teach us how to love and how to have the courage to share.

To Die Like an Angel

⁓

One evening we went out and rescued four people off the streets. One of them was in a desperate condition. I told the sisters, "You take care of the others. I will care for this one who is worse off." I did everything for her that my love could do. I put her into bed, and I saw a beautiful smile light up her face. She squeezed my hand and only managed to say two words: "Thank you." And then she closed her eyes.

I couldn't help but ask myself there beside her body, "What would I have said if I had been in her place?" My answer was very simple. I would have said that I was hungry, that I was dying, that I was cold. Or I would have said that this or that part of my body hurt or something like that. But she gave me much more. She gave me her grateful love. And she died with a smile on her face.

Just like that man we rescued from among the debris in the gutter, the one who was half-eaten by worms, this woman responded in grateful love. That man told us, "I have lived like an animal in the street, but I am going to die like an angel surrounded by love and care." It was marvelous to witness the greatness of a man who could talk like that, who could die that way without cursing anyone, without lashing out at anyone, without drawing any comparisons. He died like an angel.

Abandonment Is an Awful Poverty

⁓

One day I visited a house where our sisters shelter the aged. This is one of the nicest houses in England, filled with beautiful and precious things, yet there was not one smile on the faces of these people. All of them were looking toward the door.

I asked the sister in charge, "Why are they like that? Why can't you see a smile on their faces?" (I am accustomed to seeing smiles on people's faces. I think a smile generates a smile, just as love generates love.)

The sister answered, "The same thing happens every day. They are always waiting for someone to come and visit them. Loneliness eats them up, and day after day they do not stop looking. Nobody comes."

Abandonment is an awful poverty. There are poor people everywhere, but the deepest poverty is not being loved.

The poor we seek may live near us or far away. They can be materially or spiritually poor. They may be hungry for bread or hungry for friendship. They may need clothing, or they may need the sense of wealth that God's love for them represents. They may need the shelter of a house made of bricks and cement or the shelter of having a place in our hearts.

The Warmth of a Hand

⁓

One day I was walking down the street in London, and I saw a tall, thin man sitting on the corner, all huddled up, looking most miserable.

I went up to him, shook his hand, and asked him how he was. He looked up at me and said, "Oh! After such a long, long time I feel the warmth of a human hand!" And he sat up.

There was such a beautiful smile on his face because somebody was kind to him. Just shaking his hand had made him feel like somebody.

For me, he was Jesus in a distressing disguise. I

gave him the feeling of being loved by somebody, the joy of being loved.

Somebody loves us, too — God Himself. We have been created to love and to be loved.

∼

To Give of Yourself

⁀

One day an Australian man came and made a substantial donation. But as he did this he said, "This is something external. Now I want to give something of myself." He now comes regularly to the house of the dying to shave the sick men and to converse with them. This man gives not only his money but also his time. He could have spent it on himself, but what he wants is to give of himself.

I often ask for gifts that have nothing to do with money. There are so many other things one can give. What I desire is the presence of the donor, for him to touch those to whom he gives, to smile at them, for him to pay attention to them. All of this is very meaningful for those people.

I urge people to join our work, for our profit and for the profit of everyone. I never ask them for money or any material things. I ask them to bring their love, to offer the sacrifice of their hands. When these people run across those in need, their first move is to do something. When they come the second time, they already feel committed. After some time they feel they belong to the poor and they are filled with the need to love. They discover who they are and what it is that they themselves can give.

I think that a person who is attached to riches, who lives with the worry of riches, is actually very poor. If this person puts his money at the service of others, then he is rich, very rich.

Sharing Love with Others

~~

The other day, two friends of mine came to see me. They brought me a large amount of money to use for feeding the poor. I asked them, "Where did you get all this money?"

They answered, "We were married two days ago, but before that we had decided not to have a large wedding banquet. As a witness of our love for each other, we wanted to bring this money to Mother Teresa."

This is the greatness of young people! They are so generous! I asked them further, "Why did you do this?"

They answered, "We love each other so much, and we wanted to share our love with other people, especially with those you are serving."

⌒

The Great Gift of Love

∽

For some time now, we have had a small community of sisters in Guatemala. We came there during the earthquake of 1972 that caused so much damage.

The sisters in Guatemala came to love and serve, as they do everywhere. They told me something beautiful about a very poor man who was picked up from the city streets and brought to one of our homes. He was very sick, disabled, hungry, and helpless. But somehow, with the help he received he got well again.

He told the sisters, "I want to go and leave this

bed for somebody else who may need it as much as I needed it when I came here."

Now he has a job. I don't think he earns much, but he is working. Every time he gets a little money, he remembers the other disabled people who are in the home and comes to see them.

He always brings something for them. Even with the little he has, he always brings something.

This is the great gift of our poor people: the love they have.

⌐∽

The Tenderness of God

~⌒

*I*n Calcutta, we cook for nine thousand people every day. One day a sister came and said, "Mother, there's nothing to eat, nothing to give the people." I had no answer. And then by nine o'clock that morning a truck full of bread came to our house. The government gives a slice of bread and milk each day to the poor children at school. But that day — no one in the city knew why — all the schools were closed suddenly. And all the bread came to Mother Teresa.

See, God closed the schools. He would not let our

people go without food. And this was the first time in their lives I think, that these people had had such good bread and so much of it. This way you can see the tenderness of God.

A Home, A Gift

~~

Some young people who ran away from home have gotten sick with AIDS. We have opened a home in New York for AIDS patients, who find themselves among the most unwanted people of today.

What a tremendous change has been brought about in their lives just because of a few sisters who take care of them, and have made a home for them!

A home of love!

A gift of love!

A place, perhaps the only place, where they feel loved, where they are somebody to someone. This has changed their lives in such a way that they die a most beautiful death. Not one of them has yet died in distress.

The other day, a sister called to tell me that one of the young men was dying. But, strange to say, he couldn't die. He was struggling with death.

So she asked him, "What is it? What is wrong?"

And he said, "Sister, I cannot die until I ask my father to forgive me."

So the sister found out where the father was, and she called him. And something extraordinary happened, like a living page from the Gospel: The father came and embraced his son and cried, "My son! My beloved son!"

And the son begged the father, "Forgive me!"

Two hours later the young man died.

A Beautiful Example of Love

～

I will give you one more beautiful example of God's love. A man came to our house and said, "My only child is dying! The doctor has prescribed a medicine that you can only get in England."

We have permission from our government to store life-saving medicines that are gathered from all over the country. We have many people who go from house to house and gather leftover medicines. And they bring them to us and we give them to our poor people. We have thousands of people who come to our dispensaries.

While we were talking, a man came in with a basket of medicines. I looked at that basket: right on the top was the very medicine that man needed for his dying child! If it had been underneath, I wouldn't have seen it.

If he had come earlier or later, I would not have remembered. He came just in time.

As I stood in front of that basket I thought, "There are millions of children in the world, and God is concerned with that little child in Calcutta. To send that man at that very moment! To put the medicine right on the top, so I could see it!"

See God's tender concern for you and for me! He would do the same thing for each of you.

Generous and Great People

~⌒~

I will tell you another good example of how generous and great people are.

We had picked up a young orphan boy whose mother had died in the home for dying destitutes. She had come from a good family, but had come down in life because of difficult circumstances.

The boy grew up, and wanted to become a priest. When he was asked, "Why do you want to become a priest?" he gave a very simple answer. "I want to do for other children what Mother Teresa has done for me. I want to love as she loved me. I want to serve as she served me."

Today he is a priest, devoted to loving all those who have nothing and no one — those who have forgotten what human love is, or the warmth of a human touch, or even the kindness of a smile.

～

Prayers

"Our souls should be like a transparent crystal through
which God can be perceived.
This crystal is sometimes covered with dirt and dust.
To remove this dust we carry out
our examination of conscience,
in order to obtain a clean heart.

～ゥ

God will help us to remove that dust,
as long as we allow Him to,
if our will is that His will come about.
Our examination of conscience is the mirror
we focus toward nature:
a human test, no doubt,
but one that needs a mirror
in order to faithfully reflect its faults.
If we undertake this task with greater faithfulness, perhaps we will realize that what we sometimes
consider a stumbling block is rather
a rock we can step on."

Make Me an Instrument
of Your Peace

~

Lord, make me an instrument of your peace.
Where there is hatred, let me sow love;
   where there is injury, pardon;
   where there is doubt, faith;
   where there is despair, hope;
   where there is darkness, light;
   where there is sadness, joy.
O divine Master, grant that I may not so much seek to
be consoled, as to console;
   to be understood, as to understand;
   to be loved, as to love.

For it is in giving that we receive;
   it is in pardoning that we are pardoned;
   It is in dying that we are born to eternal life.

⚊⚊◞

Our works of love are nothing but works for peace. Let us do them with greater love and efficiency. It is always the same Christ who says:

I was hungry — not only for food but for peace that comes from a pure heart.

I was thirsty — not only for water but for peace that satiates the passionate thirst of a passion for war.

I was naked — not only for clothes but for the beautiful dignity of men and women for their bodies.

I was homeless — not only for a shelter made of bricks but for a heart that understands, that cares, that loves.

Each of us is merely a small instrument; all of us, after accomplishing our mission, will disappear.

Shine Through Me

⁓

Dear Lord, help me spread your fragrance where I go.

Flood my soul with your spirit and life.

Penetrate and possess my whole being so utterly that all my life may only be a radiance of yours.

Shine through me, and be in me, so that every soul I come in contact with may feel your presence in my soul. Let them look up and see no longer me, but only you, O Lord!

Stay with me, then I shall begin to shine as you do; to shine so as to be a light to others. The light, O Lord, will be all from you; none of it will be mine; it will be you shining on others through me.

Let me thus praise you in the way you love best, by shining on those around me.

Let me preach you without preaching, not by words but by my example, by the catching force, the sympathetic influence of what I do, the evident fullness of the love my heart bears to you.

Amen.

⌒

Don't search for Jesus in far lands — He is not there. He is close to you; He is with you. Just keep the lamp burning and you will always see Him. Keep on filling the lamp with all these little drops of love, and you will see how sweet is the Lord you love.

The fullness of our heart is expressed in our eyes, in our touch, in what we write, in what we say, in the way we walk, the way we receive, the way we serve. That is the fullness of our heart expressing itself in many different ways.

I wish to live in this world, which is so far from

God, which has turned so much from the light of Jesus, to help them — our poor, to take upon me something of their sufferings. For only by being one with them can we redeem them, that is, by bringing God into their lives and bringing them to God. Even God cannot force Himself on anyone who does not want Him. Faith is a gift.

∼

Blessed Are You Among Women

Hail Mary, full of grace! the Lord is with you;
blessed are you among women,
and blessed is the fruit of your womb, Jesus.
Holy Mary, mother of God,
pray for us sinners, now
and at the hour of our death.

When you look at the inner workings of electrical things, you often see small and big wires, new and old, cheap and expensive, all lined up. Until the current passes through them there will be no light.

That wire is you and me. The current is God. We have the power to let the current pass through us, use us, produce the light of the world. Or we can refuse to be used and allow darkness to spread.

Our Lady was the most wonderful wire. She allowed God to fill her. By her surrender — "Be it done to me according to the word" — she became "full of grace." Full of grace means full of God. The moment she was filled by this current, by the grace of God, she went in haste to Elizabeth's house to connect the wire, John, to the current, Jesus. As his mother said, "This child, John, leaped up with joy at your voice."

Let us ask Our Lady to come into our lives also and make the current use us to go round the world — especially in our own communities — so that we can continue connecting the wires of the hearts of men and women with the current of love.

With Deep Gratitude

Help me speak your fragrance wherever I go.
Flood my soul with your Spirit and life.
Penetrate and possess my whole being so utterly
that my life may only be a radiance of yours.
Shine through me and be so in me that every soul I
come in contact with may feel your presence in
my soul.
Let them look up,
and see no longer me,
but only Jesus!
Stay with me and then I will begin to shine as you

shine, so to shine as to be a light to others.
The light, O Jesus, will be all from you;
none of it will be mine.
It will be you, shining on others through me.
Let me thus praise you in the way that you love
best, by shining on those around me.
Let me preach you without preaching, not by
words but by example,
by the catching force,
the sympathetic influence of what I do,
the evident fullness of the love my heart bears
for you.
Amen.

Every day, after holy communion, my sisters and I recite the prayer above, which was composed by Cardinal Newman.

One thing I ask of you: Never be afraid of giving. There is a deep joy in giving, since what we receive is much more than what we give.

Holy, Holy, Holy

Holy, holy, holy
Lord, God of power and might,
Heaven and earth are full of your glory.
Hosanna in the highest.
Blessed is he who comes in the name of the Lord.
Hosanna in the highest.

To become holy we need humility and prayer. Jesus taught us how to pray, and He also told us to learn from Him to be meek and humble of heart. Both humility and prayer grow from an ear, mind, and tongue that have lived in silence with God, for in the silence of the heart God speaks.

Be faithful in little things, for in them our strength lies. To the good God nothing is little, because He is so great and we are so small. That is why He stoops down and takes the trouble to make those little things for us — to give us a chance to prove our love for Him. Because He makes them, they are very great. He cannot make anything small; they are infinite.

Our Father

Our Father, Who art in heaven,

hallowed be thy name;

thy kingdom come;

thy will be done on earth as it is in heaven.

Give us this day our daily bread;

and forgive us our trespasses

as we forgive those who trespass against us;

and lead us not into temptation,

but deliver us from evil.

For thine is the kingdom, the power, and the glory,

now and forever.

Amen.

The apostles asked Jesus to teach them to pray, and He taught them the beautiful prayer, "Our Father." I believe each time we say the "Our Father," God looks at His hands, where He has carved us — "I have carved you on the palm of my hand" — He looks at His hands, and He sees us there. How wonderful the tenderness and love of God!

Where can I learn to pray? Jesus taught us: "Pray like this: Our Father . . . thy will be done . . . forgive us as we forgive." It is so simple yet so beautiful. If we pray the "Our Father," and live it, we will be holy. Everything is there: God, myself, my neighbor. All this comes from a humble heart, and if we have this we will know how to love God, to love self, and to love our neighbor.

This is not complicated, and yet we complicate our lives so much, by so many additions. Just one thing counts: to be humble, to pray.

~⌒

The sisters do small things — helping children,

visiting those who are isolated, the sick, those who lack everything.

In one of the houses the sisters visit they found a woman who had died alone a few days earlier. Her body had already begun decomposing. The neighbors didn't even know her name.

When someone tells me that what the sisters do is irrelevant, that they limit themselves to things that are little less then ordinary, I reply that even if they helped only one person, that would be reason enough for their work.

~⌇

Come, Let Us Bow Down

⌒

Come, let us bow down in worship;

let us kneel before the Lord who made us.

For he is our God,

and we are the people he shepherds,

the flock he guides.

— PSALM 95:6-7

After the sisters have finished their day — carrying out their service of love in the company of Jesus, and through Jesus — we have an hour of prayer and of eucharistic adoration. Throughout the day we have been in contact with Jesus through His image of sorrow in the poor and the lepers. When the day ends, we come in contact with Him again in the tabernacle by means of prayer. The tabernacle is the guarantee that Jesus has set His tent among us.

Every moment of prayer, especially before our Lord in the tabernacle, is a sure, positive gain. The time we spend in having our daily audience with God is the most precious part of the whole day.

O Jesus, You Who Suffer

⁓

O Jesus, you who suffer,

grant that today and every day I may be able to
see you in the person of your sick ones and that,
by offering them my care, I may serve you.

Grant that, even if you are hidden under the
unattractive disguise of anger, of crime, or of
madness, I may recognize you and say, "Jesus,
you who suffer, how sweet it is to serve you."

Give me, Lord, this vision of faith,

and my work will never be monotonous.
I will find joy in harboring the small whims and

desires of all the poor who suffer.

Dear sick one, you are still more beloved to me
because you represent Christ.

What a privilege I am granted in being able to take
care of you!

O God, since you are Jesus who suffers, design to
be for me also a Jesus who is patient, indulgent
with my faults, who only looks at my intentions,
which are to love you and to serve you in the
person of each of these children of yours who
suffer.

Lord, increase my faith.

Bless my efforts and my work,
now and forever.

⁓

There are thousands of people dying for a piece of bread. There are thousands upon thousands who die for a little bit of love.

My thoughts often run to you who suffer, and I offer your sufferings, which are so great, while mine are so small.

Those of you who are sick, when things are hard, take refuge in Christ's heart. There my own heart will find with you strength and love.

If you appreciated *In the Heart of the World,*
we highly recommend the following
from New World Library:

No Greater Love

No Greater Love is the essential wisdom of Mother
Teresa — the most accessible and inspirational collec-
tion of her teachings ever published. This definitive
volume features Mother Teresa on love, prayer, giving,
service, poverty, forgiveness, Jesus, and more. It ends
with an up-to-date biography and a revealing conversation with Mother Teresa about the specific chal-
lenges and joys present in her work with the poor and
the dying.

Through her own words, *No Greater Love* cele-
brates the life and work of one of the greatest human-
itarians of our time.

The Words of Christ

In *The Words of Christ,* editor Dale Salwak distills the essence of Jesus' words from the four canonical gospels, the Acts of the Apostles, I & II Corinthians, and Revelation, and arranges them thematically.

By brilliantly presenting the heart of Christianity, *The Words of Christ* serves as a powerful reminder of the source of our traditions and of what is possible if we read and heed these words.

For the Love of God

For the Love of God presents an extraordinary group of thinkers and teachers celebrating their personal experiences of the divine.

Edited by bestselling editors Richard Carlson and Benjamin Shield, creators of *Handbook for the Soul* and *Handbook for the Heart, For the Love of God* features essays by the Dalai Lama, Andrew Harvey, Sue Bender, Matthew Fox, Rev. Michael Beckwith, Barbara De Angelis, and Marianne Williamson among others.

～

If you would like to join us in supporting the work of Mother Teresa, contact the Missionaries of Charity nearest you, or write:

The Missionaries of Charity
1596 Fulton Street
San Francisco, California 94117

～